A Victim of Boards of Directors II

BASED ON A TRUE STORY

Noie James

Inquiries and Book Orders should be addressed to:

Great Writers Media
Email: info@greatwritersmedia.com
Phone: 877-556-0487

ISBN: 979-8-89175-055-5 (sc)
ISBN: 979-8-89175-057-9 (ebk)

Contents

PREFACE

One objective for my writing this book is to expose the Boards of Directors' dereliction of duty to members at my detrimental expense. An initial complaint valued at $11,980 ended up being a multi million dollar dispute.

This book and my first one chronicle my fight for justice. I believe my books (A Victim of Boards of Directors and A Victim of Boards of Directors II) will definitely be of interest to anyone who understands what it means to persevere to right wrongs for many years.

During more than twenty years (1974 – 1995) I attained an impressive list of achievements, including in my education, career, business and excellent reputation.

I attended the University of Southern California (USC) and the University of California, Berkeley (UCB). I earned my BA degree from UCB in 1979, majoring in International Business and Finance. Then I enrolled in the two-year masters program which is ranked number seven in the United States. I earned my MBA degree in 1980, i.e. I completed the program in one year.

In 1981, I secured a management position with Hewlett-Packard (Canada) Ltd in Vancouver, British Columbia. My accomplishments included completion of a $200,000 twenty thousand square foot office renovation in four months on budget. The project included a two-thousand square foot server room to house a dedicated administration computer and peripherals. I was responsible for daily operations management including backup for a fifty port mainframe computer system.

Under my supervision, my staff managed a computer system accounting for the uses and purchases of all computer parts and equipment stored in the branch. My branch achieved a 99.8% accuracy rate in an annual inventory count. Computer inventory was valued at $750,000.

I was promoted four times from senior management in a branch office of sixty-five employees to regional management in head office for all of Canada.

After six years with Hewlett-Packard I was employed for two years in the City of Scarborough Law Department as the Director of Administration. Due to salary constraint, I chose to seek another position.

In September 1992, I was hired as Director of Finance and Administration by Marsha Sharp (CEO) for the Canadian Dietetic Association (CDA). In my first year, I achieved the following:

1. reduced third-party expenses for computer consultants' fees by 90%;
2. increased the productivity of secretarial support thereby reducing the budget for support staff by $35,000 a year;
3. increased the productivity in accounting for processing membership fee payments;
4. reduced the timeframe for updating thousands of members' personal information in the computer from six months to three weeks;
5. successfully hired a new company to produce the Association's bilingual journal on short notice.

In 1994, I had the opportunity to start my own consulting firm, i.e., M-R Consulting (MRC). I signed three contracts in the first three months. My company grossed over $183,000 in the first fifteen months of operations.

Until May 1995, my reputation among the Board of Directors was very good. I became aware of what they thought of me and my work when I participated in a Board workshop. During a break, I met with half dozen directors. One topic of discussion was the performance of the CEO. A director stated that I would be good in the position.

In June 1995, without any warning I was blindsided by serious allegations that I was acting in harmful ways to deliberately hinder the success of the projects I had been managing for a year. Suddenly, I found myself involved in a devastating fight to defend my impeccable reputation. This was the beginning of my being victimized by the Boards of Directors. My books document my effort to clear my name.

INTRODUCTION

On May 29, 1995, I was on top of the world. A year and a half later, I wanted to kill myself. I hope readers of my books will understand what drove me to the point of wanting to commit suicide. My books describe the trauma I experienced at the hands of Boards of Directors over more than twenty-five years.

I began my employment with the CDA in 1992 with a superb reputation earned over a period of twenty plus years. For some unknown reason (s) in 1995 the Board of Directors began making false allegations about my performance as a self-employed project manager and business owner.

When I failed to reach a quick settlement, I was forced to file a lawsuit. I litigated the dispute for seven and one-half years in Superior Court. The Defendants were the Canadian Dietetic Association (CDA), Dietitians of Canada (DOC) and the Canadian Foundation for Dietetic Research (CFDR).

When I could no longer afford the costs of litigation', I signed a Full and Final Mutual Release on February 3, 2003. The Defendants signed their Release on February 10, 2003.

There is currently no pending litigation or legal dispute resolution.

Unfortunately, the DOC and CFDR Boards of Directors continued to defame me after 2003. With their full Boards' approvals, a director of each Board distributed letters containing false information about me. To avoid claims of copyright infringement, I cannot print copies of their letters, which are dated and contain names of the: authors, recipient high-ranking executives (Chairman and Vice President) and multi-billion dollar corporations. Since the directors cannot deny the existence of the letters, they need to do the following: 1. Explain why they contacted two public corporations, and 2. Justify why they continued to defame me in public more than a year after they signed their Release.

For a couple of years, my mental health was quite challenged. After years of therapy, I was able to continue my fight for justice. It took me over five years to complete this book. It is supported by an appendix which includes nineteen documents proving that my claims against the Boards of Directors are irrefutable and completely refute their allegations against me and my company.

Over the years, I have been able to identify the names of directors and their responsibilities relating to this dispute between June 1995 and December 2023. I have written personal letters to many of the directors on all three Boards. The directors were named individually in my December 14, 1995 and August 31, 2017 letters.

I hope that readers of my books who may be facing what may seem like insurmountable odds are inspired to never give up, especially when they believe that they cannot survive for even one more day.

CHAPTER ONE

1995 TO 2022

In 1992, I came highly recommended as a director to the CDA. After I was hired, I more than lived up to expectations for almost two years. I impressed the Board of Directors to such an extent that they considered me as a good candidate for the position of CEO. In 1994, I was hired as a consultant by the CDA to manage projects for the CDA and CFDR.

On May 11, 1995, I completed work as the project manager for one project. The CEO took over complete control on May 12th. On May 30th, she wrote me a letter acknowledging my satisfactory completion of my work on the computer system project. See EXHIBIT FOUR. Her letter stated "…I would like to thank you for the documentation and planning that you did to focus the computer project on outstanding issues and requirements and for providing contingencies… I regret that the contract you were proposing did not turn out better."

In June 1995, I was shocked to find out that the Board of Directors was finding fault with me and my company. Unsubstantiated allegations were being lodged against me by the Board. Details of the allegations made over five years are documented in chapters four, five and six of this book. The allegations amounted to character assassination. What is a mystery is why did the Boards do it for so many years.

Maybe when the directors read my books, they will be motivated to share their reason(s) publicly. If the allegations were irrefutably true, it would mean that I committed professional suicide!

An example allegation is the following from my Superior Court records: "The Plaintiff's actions were designed to harm the CEO's reputation, frustrate attempts of the CEO to follow her mandate from the Board of Directors and to further complicate and delay completion of the computer system."

Now I ask readers to consider this fact: Between May 8 and May 30, 1995, my employee and I provided almost three hundred hours of free services to the CDA in support of the computer system project.

Even though I have felt hopeless at times, I am very grateful that I have never completely lost sight of my ultimate goal to be vindicated in the court of public opinion.

In July 1995, I hired my first of four solicitors to help me resolve the problem of my reputation being damaged by the CDA Board. I offered to settle for $11,980.79 and a board review. See EXHIBIT TEN. The Board refused my offer. See EXHIBIT TWELVE.

I hired my second solicitor to take legal action. He helped me write another letter to the next Board of Directors on December 14, 1995 requesting a board review. All except one director refused my request.

For over twenty-five years, I have been working very hard to shed light on how devastating it has been for me to lose everything dear to me through no fault of my own. The details of my specific losses are described in chapter nine of this book.

I wrote to newspaper editors at the Toronto Star and Globe and Mail in 2010 and 2019. I wrote to the DOC and CFDR directors in 2010, 2017 and 2019. I also wrote to the Boards' solicitor on December 5, 2019. See EXHIBIT NINETEEN.

The DOCs and CFDR's solicitor was sent a copy of the draft of this book. I wrote to the solicitor on January 12, 2022.

I wrote to directors and executives of the corporations that were sent letters from the DOC and CFDR Boards' directors about me.

CHAPTER TWO

CONTENT SOURCES

My books document the harmful actions of the Boards of Directors that caused damages to my reputation and business. The sources of the information and claims against the Boards between June 1995 and 2023 in my books are:

1. Boards of Directors' public records
2. Plaintiff's and Defendants' affidavits of documents
3. Plaintiff's files
4. Superior Court records
5. Internet
6. Transcripts of the Plaintiff's and Defendant's Examinations for Discovery

Chapter Three

Affidavits

The content of my three books is supported by hundreds of documents. The Boards of Directors possess over five hundred copies. Many are printed in their entirety. The names of individuals and organizations are included. See EXHIBIT TEN. Of four hundred and fifty documents listed in the Plaintiff's and Defendants' affidavits of documents, the following are referenced in my books:

- Governance policy revised February 20, 1994
- Letter April 3, 1995
- Contract 72850
- Letter of Engagement, April 4, 1995
- letter from Sharp, May 30, 1995
- Project report, October 27, 1994
- letter and project report, March 9, 1995
- final project report, March 31,1995
- contract 72167, June 1, 1995
- project report, May 8, 1995
- list of third-party invoices
- letter from Sharp, June 21, 1995
- solicitor's letter, July 7, 1995
- letter from Sharp, July 17, 1995
- business plan analysis by Mintz and Partners
- letter to CDA Board of Directors, December 14, 1995

PLAINTIFF'S FILES

- letter to DOC solicitor, 2019
- Marsha Sharp's profile
- letter to Michael H. McCain
- Full and Final Mutual Releases

- letter to Boards of Directors, March 21, 2019
- letter to Boards of Directors, August 31, 2017
- damages witness list 1995-2023
- doctors' and hospitals' patient records 1997-2023

CHAPTER FOUR

EXCULPATION

Initially, the CDA Board of Directors began making negative claims about me and my company in June 1995. Their allegations threatened to seriously harm my reputation and business. See EXHIBIT TEN.

In July, the Board refused the generous terms of the settlement offer that I proposed. In response to my lawsuit, the Board filed a statement of defense, amended statement of defense and counterclaims in Superior Court. The statements and claims were without any doubt injurious to me and my company.

Over the seven and one-half years in court, the actions of the Boards of the CDA, DOC and CFDR are best described as egregious given that everything was done in public without presenting one iota of proof of truth.

The following comparisons of the Defendant's statements to the Plaintiff's rebuttals prove that the Boards knew or should have known that the statements and claims were false.

COMPARISONS OF DEFENDANT'S STATEMENTS TO PLAINTIFF'S REBUTTALS

DEFENDANT'S STATEMENTS

In paragraph 63 of the counterclaim the Defendants stated "…the Plaintiff undertook to provide a proposal for the ongoing maintenance for the new computer system being installed at the office."

At paragraph 10 of the amended statement of defense and counterclaim Marsha stated that she requested June James to develop a plan for the ongoing administration of the system and to put it in writing for review by her.

PLAINTIFF'S REBUTTAL

Both of these statements are false. Four proposals were provided as part of the Plaintiff's contractual obligations to provide written project reports to the CEO on March 9. 'March 31, April 24 and May 8, 1995. The last proposal was Contract 72167 signed May 8th at the CEO's request. See EXHIBITS ONE, TWO, THREE and FOUR.

DEFENDANT'S STATEMENT

At paragraph 65 of the amended statement of defense and counterclaim the Defendants state "On May 30, 1995 and prior to the installation of the system the Plaintiffs without notice or cause withdrew their services."

PLAINTIFF'S REBUTTAL

The defendants paid for consulting services April 1 through May 11, 1995 per the terms of EXHIBIT SIX. Sharp swore that she was aware that the Plaintiff's staff was working at CDA "under provisions of this contract 72167."

The contract was not effective until June 1, 1995. The Plaintiff's staff worked from May 8th to May 30, 1995 for free full time. The Plaintiff worked as a consultant for free from May 12th to May 30, 1995 and signed contract 72167 on May 8, 1995.

The Plaintiff provided almost three hundred hours of free services without notice from Marsha Sharp before May 30, 1995, that she had decided not to execute contract 72167.

The Defendant's allegations in court records confirm that the Plaintiff provided services until May 30, 1995, per paragraphs of the amended statement of defense and counterclaim.

Following our meeting the Plaintiff left to speak to her staff. Later she left Sharp a voicemail message saying, "we cannot continue to work without a contract."

On May 30, 1995, Marsha wrote the Plaintiff a thank you letter. She wrote "…I regret that the contract you were proposing did not turn out better." See EXHIBIT FOUR.

At paragraph 14 of the statement of defense, the Defendant's state "the draft contract… 72167 was not executed by … any authorized employee, director or officer of the CDA at any time." Based on the foregoing information, the Defendant's statement that "the Plaintiffs without notice or cause withdrew their services" is absolutely refuted. The Defendants actually imply that the Plaintiffs were expected to continue providing free services after May 30, 1995.

The Plaintiff gave written notice on April 3, 1995. See EXHIBIT SIX. No tasks were left undone by the Plaintiff after May 11, 1995. Effective May 12th, Marsha Sharp assumed all responsibility as project manager for the computer system project.

DEFENDANT'S STATEMENT

At paragraph 68 of the statement of defense the Defendant stated "the Plaintiff's actions were designed to harm the CEO's reputation, frustrate attempts of the CEO to follow her mandate from the Board of Directors and to further complicate and delay completion of the computer system."

PLAINTIFF'S REBUTTAL

The Plaintiff's provided almost three hundred hours of free services from May 8th to May 30, 1995. They also hired an expert in local area networks to evaluate the association's network at the Plaintiff's expense.

The benefits of making these unsubstantiated allegations were that they served to exonerate Marsha Sharp and to seriously defame the Plaintiff to hundreds of directors in public.

DEFENDANT'S STATEMENT

At paragraph 69 (b) of counterclaim of statement of defense the Defendant claimed an estimated '$59,000 in damages for the Plaintiff's failure to complete the proposal for the ongoing maintenance of CDA's computer system."

PLAINTIFF'S REBUTTAL

The Plaintiff provided proposals on March 9, March 31, April 24 and May 8, 1995. See EXHIBITS ONE, TWO, THREE and FOUR. The last day that the Plaintiff was paid as a consultant was May 11, 1995. The Plaintiff was no longer under any contract with the Defendants as of May 12, 1995. In support for their claim of damages the Defendants submitted invoices for services they received from other vendors and the system developer after May 11, 1995. See EXHIBIT FIVE. The Plaintiff had no knowledge of or obligation relating to these expenses.

DEFENDANT'S STATEMENT

At paragraph 27 of the statement of defense and counterclaim the Defendants stated "…the relationship between the Plaintiffs and the CDA was terminated by the Plaintiff without notice or cause."

PLAINTIFF'S REBUTTAL

The computer system contract 72850 expired March 31, 1995. On April 3, 1995 the Plaintiff' gave written notice of termination with cause. See EXHIBIT SIX. The notice stated the Plaintiff would work until May 5, 1995 on a time and materials basis at the rate of $75 per hour.

Contract 72167 was not executed per Marsha Sharp. See EXHIBIT FOUR. Paragraph 14 of the Defendants statement of defense stated "The contract identified as service contract 72167 was not executed by Marsha Sharp."

The Plaintiff signed contract 72167 on May 8, 1995 at the Defendant's request. The Plaintiff was not obligated to provide any support after May 11, 1995. The Plaintiff's staff worked full time for free from May 8th to May 30, 1995. The Plaintiff worked full time for free from May 12th to May 30, 1995.

The free support was provided on the belief that the Defendant planned to execute contract 72167 by the end of May 1995.

On May 11th the Plaintiff and Defendant met with the system developer's president to review the Project Deficiency Report dated May 8, 1995. See EXHIBIT SEVEN. The Defendant approved the developer going $106,387 over the $50,000 budget.

For two months after I became project manager in 1994, I worked with a law firm (Hughes Etigson) to document a Software Development Agreement (SDA) and Functional Specification Document (FSD). The SDA and FSD specified in detail the contractual deliverables for Markson Skolnick Inc. The Defendants could not have hired MSI as consultants because the work they performed was not outside of the scope of their contract.

The Defendants' claim that the Plaintiffs represented that the Plaintiff's company M-R Consulting would work without a contract is ridiculous since the Plaintiff was not obligated to continue working for free after May 30, 1995.

Chapter Five

Deceitful Allegations

The CDA Board of Directors made false allegations in court records relating to the Membership project in an effort to hide the fact that the CEO breached my contract on June 14, 1995. I was used as a scapegoat.

On June 27, 1994, I signed project management contract 60374 for the CDA and CFDR.

Under the terms of the contract, I agreed to perform the work specified, i.e.:

(a)   between July 1 and July 31, 1994, document a national administrative plan specifying staff resources, shared cost, and basic operational procedures based on data received from each province;

(b)   between July 1, 1994 and March 31, 1995, review procedural documentation developed with the Membership Marketing Coordinator and Accounting Clerk;

(c)   between July 1, 1994 and March 31, 1995, act as a liaison between provincial representatives and CDA office staff;

(d)   between August 1 and December 15, 1994, coordinate the production of membership materials;

(e)   by November 30, 1994, document budget requirements for the 1995-1996 fiscal year;

(f)   by March 31, 1995, document a post-mortem report as a reference document for processing memberships in the 1995-1996 fiscal year; and

(g)   between July 1, 1994 and March 31, 1995 provide one project status update in person at the CDA head office and one written project status update to the CEO each month.

The project reports were detailed monthly reports on the progress of the specifications in the contract. These reports were status updates for current tasks, future tasks to be completed and recommendations including alternative courses of action and selection of vendors. See EXHIBIT FOURTEEN.

On March 31, 1995, the contract expired. It was replaced with the Letter of Engagement effective April 4, 1995. See the terms below (EXHIBIT ELEVEN):

"As Project Coordinator, I will handle the following tasks:

1   Chair meetings of the Working Group and provide support to complete follow-up activities identified during the meetings.

2   Monitor the status of activities assigned to team members with respect to meeting deadlines and advise the CEO of any missed deadlines.

3   By January 31, 1996, prepare a Policy Document for CDA which documents the historical development of the National Membership Management System, how the System will be maintained/updated on an ongoing basis and the decision-making process that has been agreed upon by all project participants.

4   By January 31, 1996, document an evaluation process to obtain feedback from provincial associations on the quality of and member satisfaction with services provided by CDA under the national system.

Under the contract, I worked with five people in a Working Group that reported to representatives of eight provinces and the CEO. The Working Group's mandate was to develop a national membership administrative system to support a new association after the provincial and national associations merged into one organization (now the Dieticians of Canada).

The process for the Working Group required me to take the lead in drafting documents such as the Master Plan of Action and the Policy Document. These documents would be discussed briefly at one hour teleconference meetings and would be reviewed in depth later. Based on the feedback from the Group's members, the documents were modified and then distributed to the full team for comment.

I would send out an agenda and related documents a few days before each teleconference meeting. We only had one hour to highlight the issues and make assignments for various actions. Then the individuals in the Group would review the relevant documents and respond to me in two or three weeks. Once we had reached agreement about issues and our next steps,

I would consolidate the information and send out a complete report to the full team of provincial representatives. This process worked well until June 14, 1995.

I had scheduled a meeting for May 29th. When I followed up with the Group members to ensure that they were ready for the meeting, everyone confirmed that they were ready, except for the B.C. representative. She had a conflict, so the meeting was rescheduled to June 14th. I sent the agenda and relevant documents (the draft Policy Document and documentation for the provincial evaluation process) to the Group members and to the CEO on June 9th. I did not hear back from anyone that they were not ready for the meeting.

The drafts and the updated Master Plan of Action were quite valuable because: 1) eighteen months had lapsed since the project was started, 2) the Manitoba member of the Working Group was quitting on June 30, 1995, 3) two associations still had not committed to participation in the new system, 4) the Alberta Executive Director had to make a presentation about the project to her Board of Directors and had not been involved in the project over the last year, 5) I did not have any precedents to use in drafting the Policy Document and evaluation process, 6) I would soon be replaced as Project Coordinator, and 7) it would take at least three months to reach a consensus on the document and evaluation process.

To prepare the draft Policy Document, the starting point was to review the notes from a discussion with Marsha on approximately September 14, 1994. She specified the information that should be included in the document. I then contacted each provincial representative to obtain feedback on the April 5, 1995 project update. I was responsible for the following tasks:

1)   reviewing all relevant documentation in the files going back to February 1994;

2)   following up with all provincial representatives to determine if there were any new concerns which needed to be addressed;

3)   incorporating into the Policy Document the Ontario association's performance requirements as described by the Executive Director in a memo;

4)   updating the Master Plan of Action;

5)   drafting a document that put into writing the service expectations of all of the provincial associations;

6)   and, obtaining feedback on a proposed evaluation process.

Despite the dispute with the Board about the computer system project, I didn't let it prevent me from fulfilling my obligations under the Membership contract. On June 14, 1995, I went to CDA's head office in Toronto to chair the fifth teleconference meeting with the Working Group. After I arrived, I was completely surprised when the Ontario Executive Director informed me that Marsha Sharp had cancelled the meeting without any notice to me. She did not contact me until June 21st.

Up until June 14th, I had performed well as the manager of the Membership project. There was absolutely no legitimate reason for the Board to damage my reputation and business with absolutely no proof that I had done anything wrong. The fact was that I had successfully handled all phases of the project management process with the team for a year.

Marsha's June 21st letter to me was a blatant attempt to tarnish my reputation. She claimed my work was incomplete, deficient and of little value. She simply wanted to justify having terminated my services without notice and cause.

On July 7, 1995, my solicitor wrote to the Board of Directors putting them on notice that Marsha's actions and communications could adversely impact my business. The Board was asked to investigate the details of her letters and refusal to pay for services rendered. See EXHIBIT TEN. The Board refused to take any action.

Instead, the Board made false allegations against me. The Defendants' solicitor was requested in writing to provide affidavits proving the truth of the allegations. He did not respond.

COMPARISONS OF DEFENDANTS' STATEMENTS TO PLAINTIFF'S REBUTTALS

DEFENDANT'S STATEMENT

At paragraph 61 of the statement of defense and counterclaim the Defendant stated, "without notice or cause the Plaintiffs withdrew their services from the "Membership" project resulting in delays and rework of many of the tasks which were the responsibilities of the Plaintiff's."

PLAINTIFF'S REBUTTAL

The Plaintiff did not withdraw services. The CEO cancelled the Plaintiff's services on June 14, 1995 per the CEO's letter dated June 21st.

The Plaintiff requested proof of the Plaintiff's tasks that were reworked in the absence of the Plaintiff'. The Defendant did not respond.

DEFENDANT'S STATEMENT

At paragraph 44 of the statement of defense the Defendant claimed that the Policy Document submitted by the Plaintiff had to be revised.

PLAINTIFF'S REBUTTAL

Through the Defendants' solicitor on November 28, 2000, the Plaintiff requested that a copy of the revised document be provided with an affidavit. The Defendant did not respond.

DEFENDANT'S STATEMENT

At paragraph 69(a) of the counterclaim, the Defendant claimed damages of $6,350 relating to the Membership project.

PLAINTIFF'S REBUTTAL

Through the Defendants' solicitor on November 28, 2000, the Plaintiff requested evidence supporting the claim. The Defendant did not respond.

Chapter Six

Defendants' Sworn Untruths

The Boards of Directors spent five years making false allegations against me and my company in court. Marsha Sharp (CFDR Board director) began the Defendants' Examination for Discovery. She was deposed on September 14, 2000.

As of December 5, 2000, the Defendants' solicitor refused to provide an affidavit with documents and information requested in writing on November 28, 2000 to complete the Defendant's discovery. Nevertheless, Marsha Sharp swore the following false affidavit: "… At this time, there have been no further discoveries of either party arising out of written questions and answers… I believe that discoveries in this matter are now complete."

After my deposition, I reviewed the transcript of Sharp's and the Defendants' solicitor's sworn answers to interrogatories. I wrote to the Boards of Directors identifying untrue answers for questions, including numbers 149, 150, 151, 166, 167, 216, 220, 252, 253 and 267. The directors did not respond.

COMPARISONS OF DEFENDANTS AND SOLICITOR'S ANSWERS TO PLAINTIFF'S REBUTTALS

EXAMINATION FOR DISCOVERY

Question 216

DEFENDANT'S STATEMENT

The Defendant swore that, "when the Plaintiff walked out without notice we had to manage and maintain a computer system that was not operational and not fully developed."

PLAINTIFF'S REBUTTAL

The Plaintiff provided free services of almost three hundred hours from May 8 to May 30, 1995.

Because contract 72167 was not executed, the Plaintiff had the right to stop working for free on May 30, 1995. See EXHIBIT FOUR. The Defendant was officially the project manager as of May 12, 1995.

EXAMINATION FOR DISCOVERY

Questions 252, 253

DEFENDANT'S STATEMENT

The Defendant's solicitor stated "The Plaintiff did provide service and the terms of that loose agreement – some of the terms of the proposal of the Plaintiffs were incorporated into that loose agreement … My understanding is that it was a verbal agreement between the Plaintiff and the Defendant. That the verbal agreement did in fact reflect some of the proposals in the document numbered 72167."

PLAINTIFF'S REBUTTAL

The Board of Directors have to recognize that the solicitor has been deliberately misinformed. The Governance Policy rules clearly forbid the CEO from binding the association through verbal agreements between the CEO and any person or organization. See EXHIBIT EIGHT.

EXAMINATION FOR DISCOVERY

Question 267

DEFENDANT'S STATEMENT

The solicitor swore on behalf of the Defendants "The claim we are making is that it was the withdrawal of services without notice or cause so that the Defendants were in a position of having to find other suppliers on an emergency basis almost to make up for the deficiencies of the Plaintiff's work and also to complete the work that the Plaintiff's represented that they would perform."

PLAINTIFF'S REBUTTAL

The Plaintiff gave written notice of termination April 3, 1995. See EXHIBIT SIX. The Plaintiff provided hundreds of hours of free services between May 8 and May 30, 1995. On May 30th the Defendant wrote a thank you letter to the Plaintiff'. See EXHIBIT FOUR. The letter indicated the Plaintiff was not under contract for any future work.

Problems with the quality of work performed by the system developer are thoroughly documented in the Project Deficiency Report. See EXHIBIT SEVEN.

EXAMINATION FOR DISCOVERY

Question 167

DEFENDANT'S STATEMENT

The Defendant swore that she "never signed contract 72167. We only agreed to details in the contract."

PLAINTIFF REBUTTAL

The Defendant contradicted herself in paragraph 14 of the amended statement of defense and counterclaim when she wrote "… at no time did the CEO" …verbally agree to the terms set out in service contract 72167"

EXAMINATION FOR DISCOVERY

Question 220

DEFENDANT'S STATEMENT

The Defendant stated "We had to continue with a developer (Markson Skolnick Inc.) … had "to complete some of the work on reports and this was just one example and one of the consultants we had to continue to retain to provide the services that we had expected would be provided by M-R Consulting.

PLAINTIFF'S REBUTTAL

This statement is completely false. My computer system contract extended from June 27, 1994 to March 31, 1995. The terms of the contract do not include any tasks for doing any programming. See EXHIBIT NINE.

The system developer was not a consultant. MSI was obligated to program all reports per the Software Development Agreement. See EXHIBIT SEVEN I Project Deficiencies (d).

On April 3, 1995, the Plaintiff tendered her notice of termination of the job as project manager. See EXHIBIT SIX. The Defendants paid the Plaintiff for the period April 1 through May 11, 1995 per the terms of the notice.

The Plaintiff provided general consulting support without doing any programming. See EXHIBIT TWO, Contract specification (i) and Outstanding Action Items 2) and EXHIBIT SEVEN II Outstanding Contractual Obligations (f).

CHAPTER SEVEN

BOARD PROFILES AND RESPONSIBILITIES

The website addresses for the following are:

International Confederation of Dietetic Association (ICDA)

https://www.internationaldietetics.org

Dietitians of Canada (DOC) https://www.dietitians.ca

Canadian Foundation for Dietetic Research (CFDR)

https://www.cfdr.ca

The directors have a duty to manage the organizations they represent in the best interests of the membership.

The directors' backgrounds include being: very well-educated, dedicated health professionals recognized for their accomplishments nationally and internationally, involved in research and extremely successful in their business and educational careers.

They have been and are scientists, professors, successful entrepreneurs, accomplished dietitians and of good repute. For example, see profiles in EXHIBIT SIXTEEN and EIGHTEEN for current and past directors.

Individuals who are nominated as Board directors submit their profile details which are made public so thousands of members can vote for their choices. The names of elected directors are made available to the public each year from the organizations upon request. Over the years, (1995-2022) I have obtained the names of elected directors for the CDA, DOC and CFDR Boards of Directors.

My primary source of information about the names and personal data for Board directors has been the organizations' public records. This includes phone numbers and mailing addresses (work and home). I used the information to send letters to individual directors and to follow up with phone calls which were not recorded.

In 1996, the Defendants' solicitor (O'Shea) confirmed to my solicitor that all of the directors had received my letters. He also warned that I should not contact the directors on my own. Of course, I ignored his warning, since my solicitor was helping me with the content of my letters. Later, other directors' information was used to have them served with subpoenas.

Since 1998, the names of Board directors have been available online. For example, Google the following:

1.   Who are the Board Directors for the Dietitians of Canada? Click on "more items".

2.   Who are the Board Directors for the Canadian Foundation for Dietetic Research?

On December 14, 1995, April 19, 2010 and August 31, 2017, I wrote personal letters about this dispute to over two dozen CDA, DOC and CFDR directors, including Vivian Bruce, Elizabeth Newson, Joan McLaughlin, Dr. Theresa Glenville, Gusba and Judy Sheeshka. The names of Board Directors for the Canadian Dietetic Association in 1995 and 1996 include:

Lynda Corby – President
Carollyne Conlinn – Past President
Kathleen Morpurgo – President Elect
Elma Carson – Manitoba
Carolyn Farris – Alberta
Christine Gill – Newfoundland
Martha MacLean – New Brunswick
Debbie MacLellan – Prince Edward Island
Adele McVicar – Saskatchewan
Carol O'Fallon – British Columbia
Jane Pryor – Nova Scotia
Micheline Seguin-Bernier – Quebec
Phyllis Tanaka - Ontario
Vivian Bruce
Elizabeth Newson

In 1995, the Canadian Dietetic Association was comprised of over 5,000 members who voted to elect the Board directors.. Even though the organization operated under a Policy Governance model, only one director agreed to investigate the CEO's performance in 1996

The ICDA is made up of fifty-two national associations (including the DOC) representing over 200,000 dietitian/nutritionist professionals around the world. Its role includes enhancing the image and raising awareness of the profession. Toronto, Ontario will host the International Congress of Dietetics in 2024. Marsha Sharp is a past Chair of the ICDA Board of Directors.

The Dietitians of Canada was formed in 1997. The Board of Directors has always operated under the Policy Governance model. They work within a defined set of policies and by-laws. Their roles include monitoring the CEO's compliance with boundaries, i.e evaluating the CEO's performance.

Members can access the following information about the Board's responsibilities:

1. a review of the latest priorities of the Board of Directors

2. details of the Governance Process Policy

3. Ends Policies and Executive Limitations Policies

Over 5,000 members have voted for almost one hundred directors annually in twenty-eight years. I have identified the names of the directors which has allowed me to send numerous letters to individual directors.

The key to the question "Why was my life ruined?" is that from June 1995 to 2023, the Boards of Directors failed to evaluate Marsha Sharp's performance. In addition, they have ignored the substantial amount of evidence provided about her wrongdoings.

The Canadian Foundation for Dietetic Research was created by the DOC and was incorporated in 1991 as a charitable foundation. Many corporate partnerships have been created to fund its research program. The Foundation has raised millions of dollars in donations. Marsha Sharp is a founder and has been a Board director. She has also been instrumental in spearheading fundraising drives.

Over one hundred directors have been elected to the Board since 1991. I have also identified the names, addresses and phone numbers of directors. I have written to many of these directors repeatedly to no avail.

The directors not only supported the false allegations against me, but some directors took part in defaming me to a public corporation.

The Board of Directors is responsible to the membership to protect the organization's image and reputation. I do not believe that they succeeded.

Even though the three Boards of Directors have been obligated to protect their organizations' assets and reputations, I am not aware that any directors have provided any evidence that they have done nothing wrong.

All of the Boards of Directors have developed hundreds of partnerships with large national and International corporations and institutions over the years, such as PepsiCo, Coca-Cola and Nestle' Health Science. Google the following:

1.   Who are corporate partners for the Canadian Foundation for Dietetic Research? Click on Corporate Partnerships.

2.   Who are the corporate partners of the Dietitians of Canada? Click on Dietitians of Canada & Its Industry Partners.

This is important to know when trying to understand why attacks on my reputation continued after 2003. A real conundrum is why were corporate Boards of Directors involved, when I have never met or spoken to anyone from two other corporations.

CHAPTER EIGHT

BOARDS - GUILTY OR INNOCENT?

According to Barb Anderson, past Board Chair "The principles and boundaries of Policy Governance allow the Board to take a futuristic direction and not get caught up in the details of operations."

In reality, based on my experiences, what the Policy does is provide the Boards with opportunities to avoid total accountability.

The roles of the DOC Boards are to:

- assess CEO progress on priorities

- monitor the CEO's compliance with boundaries (such as Executive Limitations) See EXHIBIT EIGHT.

- set boundaries through policies that describe conditions to be avoided by the CEO

- set Executive Limitations policies which provide the operating boundaries on matters the Board considers most important See EXHIBIT EIGHT.

Under Policy Governance, Boards that delegate to a CEO are able to hold this one position exclusively accountable. Boards should assess performance by asking the question, "Have our expectations been met?"

The results of this dispute have included:

1.   an unnecessary million-dollar dispute;

2.   wasted time in court for over seven years;

3.   a loss of credibility;

4.   individuals' and organizations' tarnished reputations.

The current Boards of Directors should investigate why this happened and how to prevent similar problems from happening again.

I am sure the Boards of Directors will want to claim that they are innocent of any wrongdoings. To prove this, they need to provide the following to support their allegations against me and my company:

1.   copies of transcripts of Board meeting minutes for 1995, 1996, 2000, 2003, 2004, 2010, 2011, 2017, 2019 and 2021 (Why: to provide evidence that the directors acted in good faith with respect to how they responded to the claims against them.)

2.   a list of the names of all directors who attended Board meetings between June 1995 and April 2022 (Why: to identify when and what steps were taken to substantiate the truth of the allegations against me.)

3.   names of directors on Boards in September 1996, September 2000 and May 2004 (Why: these individuals have personal knowledge of the accuracy of the allegations made against me publicly.)

4.   proof that the Policy Governance Executive Limitation IV E was revised after February 20, 1994 to authorize the CEO to bind the association to verbal agreements between the CEO and any person or organization (Why: as of February 20th, this was forbidden.)

5.   copies of the Software Development Agreement and Functional Specification Document (Why: the details of the SDA and FSD prove that the computer system developer could not have been hired as a consultant.)

6.   proof that the Boards of Directors did their due diligence investigating that all of the allegations, statement of defense, amended statement of defense, counterclaims, and answers during the Examination for Discovery were true and accurate.

It is a fact that the Plaintiff's claims and the Defendant's defense are mutually exclusive, I.e. it is impossible for both to be true at the same time. Consequently, I propose the following conundrum to readers:

Why did the Boards of Directors support the allegations against me?

To help readers solve this puzzle, I pose the following possibilities:

1.   The directors have proof that their defense was true and my claims were false.

2.   The directors chose to rely solely on the word of Marsha Sharp that the defense was true.

3.   The Defendants' solicitor never informed the directors about the content of the defense.

4.   The directors were never informed by Marsha Sharp about the details of the defense, including the result of the Examination for Discovery.

5.   The directors were never made aware of over four hundred documents which proved my claims against the Defendants and disproved their claims against me.

6.   The directors made no efforts to determine the truthfulness of the defense.

7.   The directors deliberately ignored evidence that the defense was false. For example, I was accused of quitting without notice or cause while the Defendants were in possession of my written notice given five weeks in advance. See EXHIBIT SIX.

8.   The directors showed a deliberate disregard for the truth.

9.   The directors never provided one iota of proof of the allegations against me.

10.   Individual directors received and rejected multiple requests to investigate the truth of allegations against me as late as March 21, 2019.

Possibilities one through five are highly improbable. Six through ten are irrefutable. Consequently, the solution to the puzzle is that there is no legitimate reason for the Boards of Directors to have supported the claims against me. The question of guilt or innocence has only one logical answer.

CHAPTER NINE

LIFETIME OF DAMAGES

The Boards of Directors might be tempted to claim Marsha Sharp should bear most of the blame for the damages I suffered. As a director of one of the organizations being sued, she was in a unique position to control the Boards' acceptance of false claims against me. She was also the CEO reporting to the other two organizations.

Marsha was the only possible source of derogatory information provided to the three Boards of Directors about me and my company. She has undoubtedly been a powerful individual, who has been in several positions that provided her with significant opportunities to influence the attacks on my reputation in public documents.

She has had influential relationships with hundreds of Board members and hundreds of thousands of dietitians/nutritionists on an international level. See EXHIBIT EIGHTEEN.

Nevertheless, all of the Boards of Directors have to be held accountable for the damages to my reputation, business, physical health and mental well-being.

I have suffered ongoing damages to my reputation up to 2023. Hundreds of new Board directors have been elected between 1995 and 2023. The Board directors are responsible for orienting new members each year. This includes reviewing the status of serious claims like mine against the organizations.

On May 29, 1995, I had everything to live for, including a family life that was as perfect as could be. I had been happily married to my husband for twenty-four years. My twenty-year-old son was finishing law school at Queens University. My daughter was doing well in private school. My career and business were super successful. My home was almost mortgage free. My husband and I enjoyed many long weekends spending time in Stratford, Ontario. We were aficionados of Shakespeare plays.

I had an excellent profession as a public speaker. During my eight years that I was involved with Toastmasters International, I had been very successful utilizing my leadership skills. When I joined my club in Oakville, Ontario, I was able to make some important business connections. After I achieved my first designation in public speaking, I became an excellent mentor for new members as President of my club. After I was elected as Area Governor, I was able to get more involved in the district planning level for international events. I was living a dream. My business was very successful because I was able to work very long hours every day.

As of May 31, 1995, Sharp was having trouble performing as project manager for the computer system project. She decided her solution was to blame the Plaintiff for a myriad of problems. I not only lost my excellent reputation, but future meaningful related employment and business opportunities were virtually eliminated because I could not document thirty-three months of excellent work experience and corresponding very good references.

I lost my decade's long marriage because of my reaction to everything that happened to me. My daughter's life was seriously disrupted, because her secure family life was torn apart. I suffered from severe depression. I was utterly and thoroughly defeated, because I could not understand why everything I had before May 30, 1995 had been taken away from me. No amount of money will ever make-up for my loss of my will to live.

The whole situation with my dispute just became more than I could bear. I was driven to wanting to commit suicide. I tried to find a place to buy cyanide to poison myself, but I was unsuccessful. Finally, I decided to kill myself with my husband's gun. I drove to Lake Ontario with his gun in my lap. I sat in the empty parking lot on a rainy evening for hours sobbing uncontrollably. I was torn between being a faithful Catholic and ending the crushing HELL I was being put through on a daily basis. Finally, I decided to write a suicide letter and to take it to my physician Dr. De Grout. He sent me to the Oakville/Trafalgar hospital where I was seen by Dr. Girgla, the on-duty psychiatrist. I gave him my suicide letter to read. I explained why I was there over about an hour crying hysterically. He asked me for my phone number and called my husband to come to the hospital. When he arrived, Dr. Girgla showed him my letter and explained his diagnosis. Dr. Girgla prescribed medication for me and took me on as an outpatient. I was in therapy for years under three psychiatrists.

For a while, I was committed to the hospital's locked psychiatric ward. I was having a very difficult time dealing with my divorce and the loss of my home. At the same time, the Defendants were making egregious attacks on my reputation causing me intentional emotional distress. I still take anti-depressants daily.

As a result of my divorce, my home had to be sold. I did much of the preparation work myself. In 1997, I tried to lift a fifteen-foot pole out of the ground using a pick axe. I stopped trying when I felt a sharp pain in my back. My doctor did not diagnose the true cause of the pain. I was on pain medicine for years without knowing what was wrong.

In 2012, I began having trouble walking. In 2013, I became paralyzed from the waist down. I was taken to the hospital. My x-ray showed damage to my spine, the doctors did not diagnose the cause of my paralysis. Surgery was suggested. I refused because of the risk that I could end up totally paralyzed. I was sent to a rehabilitation hospital for two months. Then I was moved to a homecare facility.

The following information is from my doctors' and hospitals' patient records. It is a brief summary of what happened to me after I was admitted to my third long-term care facility on September 8, 2018.

Because I was suffering excruciating pain in my back, I was taken by ambulance to the emergency departments of multiple hospitals.

On December 6, 2018, I was sent to Mount Sinai hospital. I was examined and sent home without a diagnosis as to the source of my pain.

On January 14, 2019, I was sent to Mount Sinai hospital again. The doctor ordered a CT scan. I was sent home again without a diagnosis as to the source of my pain.

On February 14, 2019, my doctor arranged for me to be examined by a pain consultant. She concluded that the source of my pain stemmed from a problem with my spinal cord.

On March 7, 2019, I was sent to the emergency department of Michael Garron hospital. There are no words to express the extreme helplessness I felt while awaiting my transfer out of the emergency waiting area. A doctor attending to a patient next to me heard me cry out in pain. He turned to me and said "It's strange that you complain just when a doctor comes near you." I had been waiting to be examined for more than an hour and a half.

When I was finally examined, I was admitted to the hospital. The doctor brought in a neurologist to examine me. She only confirmed that I had no feeling below my waist. On March 12, 2019, I was discharged without a diagnosis as to the source of my pain.

In June 2019, I was sent to the Lyndhurst Centre site of the Toronto Rehabilitation Institute that specializes in treating patients with spinal cord injuries. After examining me, the doctor arranged for me to get an MRI x-ray. I had it on June 23, 2019 at the Toronto Western hospital.

After the doctor received the results, he was able to diagnose the source of my pain, i.e. in 1997, I had suffered a herniated disc in my vertebrae. He recommended that I have surgery immediately. I declined because of the high risk of ending up being totally paralyzed. Instead, I opted to continue controlling my pain with the narcotic hydromorphone administered every four hours as needed. It was prescribed for me from January 2019 through November 2022. In December, I was switched to a different pain medication.

Due to a new complication, I became unable to sit up. I have been bedridden since 2021.

The heartbreaking reality of my situation is that I succumbed to the pressure of having to deal with the false allegations made against me for years. If I had not experienced a mental collapse, my marriage would not have ended and I would not have had to sell my home. I would not have been injured. and WORST OF ALL, I would not be experiencing an extremely poor quality of life as a bedridden paraplegic today.

The organizations are liable for general damages of $150, 000,000 US. Their solicitor was advised in writing of the settlement amount on December 5, 2019 and in January 2022.

Specific general damages caused by the action of defamation by at least two hundred directors on three Boards of Directors over twenty-eight years are:

1.   mental health problems - psychiatric collapse and severe depression

2.   loss of consortium: i.e. loss of the benefits of a twenty-four year marriage relationship

3.   emotional distress

4.   physical pain: complications from the insertion of a catheter for over ten years, as well as ongoing spinal cord pain

5.   disability- paralysis

6.   reduced quality of life

7.   future pain and suffering - twenty-five more years of spinal pain and living as a bedridden paraplegic 24/7 in a 150 square foot room that I am in now.

My claim for the damages I have suffered over the past twenty-eight years is supported between 1995 and 2023 by my patient records from multiple doctors and hospitals, as well as many witnesses (including solicitors).

My witnesses include the following:

1.   W. Alex Kyle (solicitor) who provided both legal and moral support from the beginning of this dispute

2.   John Razulis (solicitor) who represented me for years in Superior Court. He personally copied hundreds of affidavit documents which he filed in Superior Court and delivered to the Defendants' solicitor O'Shea.

3.   Dr. Francis James (ne Buzaid) who witnessed my mental breakdown which caused the breakup of my marriage

4.   Dr. Girgla who is the first of three psychiatrists that treated me when I became suicidal

5.   Dr. De Grout who committed me to the Oakville/Trafalgar hospital's psychiatric ward

6.   Alan James (solicitor) who became my guardian while I was committed

7.   Sharon Williams who 1. arranged for the removal of the pole I tried to lift out of the ground with a pick ax when I hurt my spine and 2. assisted in getting me released from the psychiatric ward

8.   John Carter who rented logging equipment to remove the pole from my backyard

9.   Dr. Birmingham who has been my primary physician since 2019

The directors' actions to defame me have been relentless for twenty-eight years. Their behavior has not aligned with their priorities and strategic plans which include: "1. promoting the Dietitians of Canada's principles of professional practice by acting with honesty, accountability and reliability; and 2. assuring the organization's sustainability for members: by

(i) ensuring the focus on cost reduction and (ii) providing responsible stewardship of all resources including members' dues."

If I live for another twenty-five years, I will continue to experience a heartache that hasn't healed to date, i.e. overwhelming grief for the loss of my decades-long marriage.

Finally, I am tortured everyday by constant reminders of the fact that I would never have suffered any damages if my offer to settle for $11,980.79 and a board review had not been rejected by the Board of Directors for the Canadian Dietetic Association on July 17, 1995. See EXHIBITS TEN and TWELVE.

CONCLUSION

My success in my education, career and business were very much due to my willingness to work very hard seven days a week. My significant rewards for my achievements over twenty plus years included having earned an exceptionally good reputation.

So, it is understandable that in July 1995, I quickly took steps to protect my good name. This was necessitated by the CDA Board of Directors' CEO engaging in actions in June that seriously jeopardized my reputation and consulting business. The Board of Directors made numerous serious and unfounded allegations against me and my company in public records, none of which were ever proven to be true.

I was unable to go to trial after seven and a half years in court. I did however continue trying to vindicate myself for twenty more years.

When you consider the fact that if the Board of Directors had done a thorough and fair investigation of the dispute on July 7, 1995, you realize that my life would not have been ruined and my reputation would not have been destroyed. I have proven that the Boards' allegations were not true and that they should be held accountable for the consequences of their actions.

The Boards of Directors were given a significant amount of time to review the content of this book. Their solicitor was couriered a complete copy two years ago. Since then, no one has ever denied or objected to any information in it.

The irony of this situation is that directors on the 1993/1994 Board of Directors took their roles under the Policy Governance model very seriously, especially with respect to evaluating Marsha Sharp's (CEO) performance. The Board took unprecedented steps to define for Marsha what it meant for the CEO to be accountable to the Board of Directors. Unfortunately, by 1995 with changes in directors, the Board relinquished control in some important areas of Marsha's performance. The Board did not ensure that performance reports from Marsha were substantiated with indisputable facts. This was a major change from the 93/94 Board.

Without any proof that I did anything wrong, a million-dollar question will remain for all time. It is "For what reason(s) were false allegations made against me publicly?" The answer(s) will be the Boards' legacy forever.

I believe with all my heart in fighting for justice. The success of this book will mean that I will finally be victorious.

Now that you have finished reading my book, hopefully you have formed an opinion about whether or not you believe the Boards of Directors have been guilty of wrongdoings. You are encouraged to share your thoughts with the author and the Boards of Directors.

For example, if you decide they were in the wrong, you might think that they should make amends, and if so, how. For example, by vote of the members and/or in accordance with rules of any applicable by-laws replace all of the current Boards of Directors in 2024 with new first-time directors charged with responsibility for performing the following tasks: 1) resolving why this situation was allowed to escalate out of control so horribly wrong for so many years, and 2) implementing effective measures and policies that ensure it never happens again in the future.

I can be contacted at

victimofboards2@gmail.com

The Boards of Directors can be contacted by mail, phone, email and internet as follows:

By mail –

1. Board Chair
Dietitians of Canada

2. Canadian Foundation for Dietetic Research Secretariat
99 Yorkville Avenue
Second Floor
Toronto, Ontario M5R 1C1
Canada

By phone – in English au en Francais

1. 877 721 0876
2. 416 642 9309

By email –

1. board@dietitians.ca

By website:
2. www.cfdr.ca

Appendix

Exhibit One

Effective April 1, 1995, I worked on the computer system project on a time and materials basis. On March 9th, I produced a project status report for the CEO.

"March 9, 1995

…

Dear Marsha:

The attached report is an interim report on the progress to date regarding the computer system development project covered by contract 72850. The report also includes information on the activities which must be completed after this contract ends on March 31st, and alternatives for handling ongoing system management functions.

I will provide a final project report on March 31st. It will include information on any outstanding tasks which must be completed by" the developer.

Sincerely,

June James

Consultant"

"Interim Progress Report: The Canadian Dietetic Association

Date – March 9, 1995

Contract Number 72850

Project – Computer System

Consultant – June James

Contract specification: (b)

Between July 1 and November 30, 1994, act as liaison between CDA and Markson Skolnik Inc. during the initial programming phase of this project.

MSI still expects to complete the programming by March 20th. After that date programming tasks will be related to making changes to the "computer system" as requested by the staff during the acceptance test."

As a follow-up to the February 27th meeting with MSI, I checked my notes regarding the capability to perform random sorts. ...This requirement can be met without having MSI perform additional programming. The Systems Analyst should be able to use Oracle's query builder to create a random number generator.

Future budgets should include money for the system enhancements, if they cannot be programmed by the Systems Analyst. Additional programming will be required for the following system enhancements:

1)   a "soundex" feature

2)   a "Personnel": menu item (To date MSI has not agreed to include this as part of the development of "the computer system" at no extra charge.)

3)   the capability to create a report and mark individual data items for deletion or to be saved as a new group using a single command, and

4)   the capability to automatically update the federal/provincial Riding fields based on postal codes for members' home addresses. "A postal code file in ASCII, comma delimited format can be purchased from a third party and loaded into the "computer system" after the programming is complete."

Contract specification: (f)

Direct the Systems Analyst in developing a complete user guide based on CDA's internal operational procedures.

Patricia, Georgette and I met by teleconference on March 6th to review drafts of the procedures related to membership renewals. Their procedures will be revised to make them consistent. When I receive the revisions, I will arrange to meet with" MSI's Systems Analyst "to discuss the User Manual. I have let him know that the manual must be completed prior to CDA signing off on the computer system."

Mary's and Roberte's procedures for processing insurance and network applications and payments are probably adequate for someone who knows how to perform the job functions. I will meet with Patricia on March 16th to discuss suggestions for steps the staff can take to improve their documentation. They can:

1)   review other staff's related procedures to ensure consistency.

2)   test procedures for clarity and sufficient detail by having someone who is unfamiliar with jobs try to perform the tasks without assistance.

3)   identify "best practices" for writing procedures. They could work as a group, or Patricia could guide this activity.

(Currently, there are differences in the format, content and detail for the various procedures.)

Word Perfect files will be transferred to the on-line databases at a later date. I have recommended that this be handled by CDA's Systems Analyst because it is unlikely that MSI's analyst will have time to work on this task.

…

OTHER ACTION ITEMS

NOTE: Responsibility for the activities listed below will have to be assigned to someone.

1)   The staff need to complete the data entry for policies, file retention records and operational procedures. Additional programming will be required to create new on-line databases.
…

2)   After the staff have had an opportunity to generate reports using MSI's Report Router and Oracle's SQL, the Systems Analyst should determine if there is a need to purchase software that is easier to use, such as Excel. New software may not be required, since MSI is modifying its Report Router.

3)   Decisions are required regarding external access to the national database. In general, external users of the system (staff and volunteers in provincial associations) should be limited

to "read only" access, but it may be appropriate for them to update certain data. This will have to be evaluated when their security is set up.

4)   A plan needs to be developed for adding the provincial associations' computerized and manual records to the national system. The plan should address the provision of training and support to external users.

5)   A decision is needed on the disposition of the data from the 1994 member survey. I have spoken to MSI. If the information is going to be uploaded, it should be done during the period that MSI is providing operational support.

6)   I have asked MSI to provide an updated quotation for an annual support contract. ...I will review their agreement and give you a recommendation.

7)   Responsibility needs to be assigned for the Information Systems management and development activities. These job functions are normally handled by someone other than the Systems Analyst. ...the goal should be to work toward combining these two jobs.

I have listed the job responsibilities of the Information Systems Manager and the Systems Analyst for your information.
...

Option 2

It is possible to hire a full time Systems Analyst for $35,000 - $40,000 per year. These individuals usually have limited work experience and will probably require a great deal of supervision in the beginning. If you choose this option, I suggest that you register with college and university placement centers. A senior analyst will cost between $55,000 and $70,000 per year.

Option 3

In order to determine if this option is suitable for the Systems Analyst position, a decision has to be made regarding the minimum number of hours of support that will be required for CDA to run its operations effectively.

(a)   Support services can be obtained from MSI at the rate of $85 per hour on a time and materials basis.

(b)   There are companies that specialize in providing contract staff to fill Information Systems positions. The hourly rate for an experienced Systems Analyst with programming skills would range from $35 - $55 per hour.

(c)   My company can provide a Systems Analyst for two days (14 hours) a week at the rate of $45,000.00 per year. The cost of a contract covering the period June 1, 1995 through March 31, 1996 would be $37,500.00. If the contract can be billed in advance on the first of each month, June to March, I can provide a Systems Analyst for 88 hours during the month of May 1995 at no charge to CDA.

My first choice for this position is Dave Marsh. I have attached his resume for your reference. He will have to take a programming course in Oracle (at our expense). CDA managers would not have to provide supervision under this alternative.

As we discussed, several of the decisions that have to be made in the short term will be influenced by three factors: 1) staff competence, 2) member expectations and 3) costs.

Staff Competence

In addition to training staff on the use of hardware and software applications, it will be important to focus on maintaining the integrity of data at the user level. ...

Member Expectations

A communications plan needs to be developed around CDA's implementation of new information systems. ... A plan is needed to ensure that members' expectations are set properly regarding their access to information systems, availability of services and implementation timeframes. ...

Implementation Costs

The implementation of new information systems and services will require an ongoing commitment of funds for staff support (technical and management), long distance and data transmission charges, telephone lines and service bureau fees. Variables that will affect the amount of total expenditures are the number of users, connect time and the amount of data transmitted. Once the commitment has been made to an IT initiative, its success will require a sustained financial investment.

The next step would be to document a proposal to the Board for specific funding over three years for the development and implementation of a national Information Systems and

Technology Infrastructure. The proposal should include: 1) a long-term Information Systems management and development plan and 2) a business plan that identifies means of recovering costs and possibly generating future profits.

This project should be contracted out to a consultant. A company such as P.J. Ward and Associates could provide a qualified consultant to prepare these plans. Tom Bradshaw of Lateral Technology has indicated that he would be willing to provide a quotation. My cost for my company to handle this project would be $37,500.00. In addition to developing the plans, we would also provide one month of on-site assistance in August for the initial implementation.

Exhibit Two

" Final Project Report: The Canadian Dietetic Association

Date – March 31, 1995

Contract Number – 72850

Project – Computer System Development

Consultant – June James

Contract specification: (f)

Direct the Systems Analyst in developing a complete User Manual based on CDA's internal operational procedures.

Sean Hunt and I will be meeting on April 10th to review his draft notes for the User Manual and to discuss the related operational procedures. I will review the manual as work progresses during April. The staff will use it during the acceptance test to ensure that there are no major omissions which will prevent you from signing off on the' computer system.

"Contract specification: (h)

Assist with application testing using the entire database after conversion.

I will provide support for testing the system until it is accepted. I am planning to run each of the reports listed on my fax dated February 15th and to print all of the tables. Where necessary, I will enter dummy information into the system where appropriate, e.g., to test the survey function. …The testing is scheduled to be completed April 27th, at which time the staff should be able to use the new system exclusively. If they are able to use the system for five consecutive business days without encountering any significant problems, the system can be signed off by May 5th. …

Contract specification: (i)

Identify specifications for standardized reports to be created by the Systems Analyst.

I recommend that some of the less complex reports be programmed by the Systems Analyst after the system is accepted. MSI has had to add two new staff to the project in order to complete the programming for reports. I will be meeting with the staff on April 4th to review each report that MSI will deliver for testing. One or both of the programmers will meet with the CDA and Ontario association staff as soon as I can arrange it."

The developer encountered significant problems with the programming of reports. The primary reasons were problems with the old version of software. These problems had not been resolved by May 11th; the last day I was paid for work I did for the association. According to a letter dated May 30, 1995 from Marsha the report programming problems still had not been eliminated. (See EXHIBIT FOUR).

As of May 12th, Marsha took over as Project Manager for the computer system project. Yet, at question 216 of the Examination for Discovery, she lied under oath when she stated "…they walked out without notice" (they being the Plaintiffs on May 30, 1995) … Damages were caused because "we had to invest time in the report development … and we had to find without any notice people to manage and maintain a computer system that was not operational …" Because of the Plaintiffs actions a great deal of "…re-work and delays were introduced."

Since the Defendants did not execute contract 72167 and the Plaintiffs did not agree to work for free past May 31, 1995, the Plaintiffs cannot be held accountable for services delivered by the developer and other vendors after May 11, 1995. At question 220 of the Examination for Discovery, the CEO stated, "… We had to continue with a developer. … Markson Skolnik" had "to complete some of the work on reports and this was just one example and one of the consultants we had to continue to retain to provide the services that we had expected would be provided by M-R Consulting." The Defendants had no basis to expect the Plaintiffs to continue to provide services after May 31, 1995 without a contract.

"OUTSTANDING ACTION ITEMS – March 31, 1995

1) A timetable needs to be created to have work related to the system tables completed. The list of code tables in the Functional Specification Document is not complete. It should also include: account type, company type, department type (CDA's), institutions (university/hospital), order status, output device group, product status and publication period. … The work falls into categories.

(a) <u>Create new table codes</u>

The existing staff team can coordinate the creation of codes and Systems Analyst can enter the information. Presently, there are no plans to use the account type and department type tables. Decisions are needed on codes for the following tables:

(i) previously listed: contact type, continuing/advanced education category, ethnicity, group type,

(ii) not previously listed: company type, order status, product status and publication period.

(b) <u>Correct and revise existing table codes:</u>

The existing staff team can also coordinate the decision-making process for making changes and additions to the codes for the following tables: city, country, degree type, employer type, language, position type, province and sector of employment.

It would be advisable to involve one of the original programmers because the sequence of changes is important as some tables reference other tables.

2) MSI has to complete the following tasks by the dates specified:

— the programming for reports, the posting procedures and the system enhancements that have been requested, by April 20th so that the final conversion can be completed by April 24th

— documentation of the User Manual by April 24th to allow enough time for the staff to test it and for MSI to make any necessary changes.

Following Tom Bradshaw's review of the computer system on April 20th, we will decide if the SPD systems will have to be used to process renewals beginning April 21st. I will work with Mary and Patricia next week to identify and plan for the steps that must be taken prior to the 21st so that SPD can be used immediately, if necessary.

The computer system currently does not accommodate overseas phone numbers. I will obtain a quote for the programming.

3) MSI does not sell support agreements for custom applications. CDA will either obtain support from MSI under the terms of the eighteen-month warranty or on a time and materials basis at the rate of eighty-five ($85) dollars per hour.

I have attached a draft of the contract "72167" for my company to provide a Systems Analyst for CDA. Dave Marsh has accepted another position. If I cannot confirm who will be filling this job by April 10th, I will provide the individual's resume for your approval and arrange for a meeting when you return to the office."

Exhibit Three

On April 24, 1995, I wrote to Marsha regarding the continuance of my support. I also rescinded my contract proposal 72167. The letter read:

"April 24, 1995

…

Dear Marsha:

As of April 22nd, my hours worked equaled the number of hours budgeted for consulting support for testing the computer system. Tom has provided approximately an additional ten hours to test the system and generate reports from SPD. Presently, I do not anticipate that we will need his services for further testing; however, he should certify the deliverables specified in Schedule C of the Development Agreement, specifically, items 3a, b, c, d, e and 4.

I have prepared a status report on the system implementation for you and Mary Ann. Please advise me if you wish me to continue providing support until May 5th, assuming the computer system is accepted by that date. All of the activities identified in the status report do not necessarily need to be performed and/or supervised by me. I recommend that you and Mary Ann take over working with the individual staff during the week of May 1st. This would provide two important benefits, i.e., minimize additional expenses for my services, and provide both of you with the information that you will need to make realistic assessments of your ongoing support needs for the balance of the year.

Based on my experience during the implementation, I do not believe that part-time support is appropriate. Consequently, I will not be pursuing my previous contract proposal 72167. When you and Mary Ann, have identified your requirements, I would be pleased to submit a competitive bid for the contract, if you wish me to do so. I would appreciate it if you could let me know what you plan to do by May 5th …

Sincerely,

June James

Consultant"

I withdrew my contract proposal 72167 because the staff required more individual support than I wanted to provide. Marsha and I discussed my concerns in her office on the evening of April 25th.

We discussed problems with the training that the developer's Systems Analyst was providing to the staff. Marsha accepted my recommendation in my April 24th status report that she pay to have one of the programmers take over the training. She wrote out a plan and gave the handwritten training schedule to me to implement the training on April 26th. Marsha lied at paragraph 11 in the Amended Statement of Defence and Counterclaim where she stated she "… did not have discussions with June James between April 24, 1995 and May 1, 1995." She also lied under oath, during her deposition at question 144 when she stated that "… I requested" a training plan "of June James."

Marsha also accepted my recommendation on April 25th to "Engage M-R Consulting to inspect the entire network configuration and correct any deficiencies prior to accepting the system. An individual certified by Novelle as an expert will perform the work" at my expense. "The purpose of this is to minimize the chance of encountering major problems with the network soon after the system has been accepted."

Exhibit Four

The letter from the CEO to the plaintiff dated May 30, 1995 does not reflect any work left undone by the plaintiff or significant problems caused by the plaintiffs declining to continue to work for free without a signed contract.

The CEO wrote in her letter that, "I would like to thank you for the documentation and planning that you did to focus the computer project on outstanding issues and requirements and for providing for contingencies. We did make the decision to install the new version of forms software and we did have "the programmers" redo all the forms in the system. Work on reports is progressing, although more slowly than hoped.

... I regret that the contract you were proposing did not turn out better."

MARSHA SHARP swore at question 167 of her Examination for Discovery that she "never signed contract 72167. We... agreed to details in the contract."

EXHIBIT FIVE

At questions 252 and 253 of the transcript for the Examination for Discovery, the Defendants' solicitor stated "… the Plaintiffs did provide service to the CDA and the terms of that loose agreement – some of the terms of the proposal of the Plaintiffs were incorporated into that loose arrangement. … My understanding is that it was a verbal agreement between June James and Marsha Sharp but that verbal agreement in fact did reflect some of the proposals in the document numbered 72167."

At paragraph 69(b) of the Counterclaim, the Defendants claimed an estimated $59,000.00 in damages "for the Plaintiffs' failure to complete the proposal for the on-going maintenance of the CDA's computer system."

Dozens of invoices were submitted by the Defendants in support of their claim. The invoices were for work requested by Marsha Sharp in addition to the computer system developer's original contract. The original contract price was $50,000.00. The additional billing was $106,387.18 for system enhancements, programming the source code, debugging the completed application and training the staff on new, added and amended system functions. The Plaintiffs had no knowledge or control over the work completed by the developer and other vendors after May 11, 1995.

If service contract 72167 had been executed by Marsha Sharp, it would have expired on March 31, 1996. The defendants claimed damages for work completed after March 31st, e.g., invoice 703557 dated March 19, 1997 was for general support from the developer.

The following vendors were hired without the knowledge of the Plaintiffs:

Nu Connexions	Invoice #96001	May 6, 1996	2953.20
Nu Connexions	Invoice #96003	June 28, 1996	2974.60
Nu Connexions	Invoice #96004	July 30, 1996	5797.60
Nu Connexions	Invoice #96005	Aug. 30, 1996	3509.60
Nu Connexions	Invoice #96006	Sept. 30, 1996	3338.40
Nu Connexions	Invoice #96007	Oct. 31, 1996	3060.20
Nu Connexions	Invoice #96008	Nov. 30, 1996	3289.60
Nu Connexions	Invoice #96009	Dec. 31, 1996	1442.80

Nu Connexions	Invoice #97001	Jan. 31, 1997	3351.25
Nu Connexions	Invoice #97002	Feb. 28, 1997	3490.80
Nu Connexions	Invoice #97003	March 31, 1997	299.60
Nu Connexions	Invoice #97004	April 29, 1997	460.10
Nu Connexions	Invoice #97005	July 16, 1997	160.50
Market Link	Invoice 1708	Jan. 15, 1997	5403.50
Market Link	Invoice 781	Feb. 27, 1997	35197.65
Market Link	Invoice 796	March 27, 1997	20000.44
Market Link	Invoice 911	June 30, 1997	19167.61
Goodman And Carr	Account 268538	Aug. 28, 1997	11621.68
Des Tech	Invoice CDA970531	May 31, 1997	3638.00

Marsha incurred the following expenses after I was no longer Project Manager for the computer system:

Lateral Technology	Invoice 1205	May 31, 1995	341.06
Lateral Technology	Invoice 1211	June 30, 1995	160.50

Markson Skolnik Inc. (developer) GST excluded

Invoice 505204	May 20, 1995	5850.00
506217	June 24, 1995	3500.00
506218	June 24, 1995	3300.00
506219	June 24, 1995	3186.23
506220	June 24, 1995	1635.00
506229	July 26, 1995	1290.00
507230	July 26, 1995	2630.40
507231	July 26, 1995	2925.00
509249	Sept. 4, 1995	2742.50
509250	Sept. 4, 1995	1377.50
509251	Sept. 4, 1995	1355.40
509255	Sept. 4, 1995	2081.25
510272	Oct. 7, 1995	425.00
510273	Oct. 7, 1995	3147.06
510274	Oct. 7, 1995	1211.63
510288	Oct. 22, 1995	2169.56
511311	Nov. 27, 1995	5074.50
512319	Dec. 10, 1995	4694.50
512323	Dec.11, 1995	1394.12
601331	Jan. 14, 1996	3105.75
602352	Feb. 11, 1996	7249.00

603364	March 9, 1996	4267.25
604375	April 13, 1996	3871.75
605386	May 20, 1996	4886.88
605392	June 1, 1996	8367.38
607501	July 10, 1996	3831.00
608509	Aug. 28, 1996	2588.00
609517	Sept. 7, 1996	2142.75
610524	Oct. 14, 1996	7523.00
611531	Nov. 12, 1996	347.25
612537	Dec. 15, 1996	234.25
703557	March 19, 1997	998.50

Exhibit Six

On April 3, 1995, I gave the CEO notice about terminating my job as Project Manager for the computer system project. I attached my final project status report and a proposal to provide a Systems Analyst to support the system and users. The support proposal was the first contract 72167.

"April 3, 1995

…

Dear Marsha:

Attached is the final report on work performed on CDA's computer system development project covered by contract **72850.** I have included information on job tasks which must be handled by CDA staff or contract personnel, the outstanding work which must be completed by MSI and updates for some of the action items listed in my last interim project report on March 9th.

In the future, I will provide services on a time and materials basis at the rate of seventy-five ($75) dollars per hour. At the present time, I am planning to provide support for a maximum of 125 hours up to May 5th. …

Please let me know if you require any additional information or have questions.

Sincerely,

June James, MBA

Consultant"

Even though I gave notice of my termination as Project Manager more than a month in advance and provided a support contract proposal almost two months in advance, Marsha lied in the Defendants' Amended Statement of Defence and Counterclaim. She stated at paragraph 9 "… discussions concerning the ongoing and future administration of the computer system … were suspended during the month of April …" At paragraph 10 she stated that she requested "June James to develop a plan for the ongoing administration of the system and to put it in writing for review by" her. At paragraph 65 she stated that "On May 30, 1995, and prior to the successful installation of the system, the Plaintiffs, without notice or cause, withdrew their services …" This was a lie since I had been working for the association for free from May 12 through May 30, 1995.

In the Examination for Discovery at question 151, Marsha admitted that "there was no plan. There was what you've called service contract 72167…"

My last project report anticipated that the computer system would be programmed and accepted by May 5, 1995.

Exhibit Seven

The Project Report is as follows:

"IMPLEMENTATION OF DATABASE MANAGEMENT SYSTEM APPLICATION AND LOCAL AREA NETWORK

Date: **May 8, 1995**
Client: **The Canadian Dietetic Association**
Vendor: **Markson Skolnik Inc.**
Consultant: June James, M-R Consulting

I. Project Deficiencies

As of May 5, 1995, the AMS could not be accepted by the Canadian Dietetic Association due to the existence of the following deficiencies:

(a)   The inventory Order Entry form does not allow users to enter "Ship To" or "Bill To" addresses for orders. At the present time, CDA is unable to use this function.

(b)   The LAN installation is incomplete and to date has not worked satisfactorily. AccPac has not been installed on the network. Staff are able to print from WordPerfect 6.1 by way of a temporary fix that has been implemented. This needs to be resolved on a permanent basis. Items B2 through B11 under LAN REQUIREMENTS on pages two and three of the fax dated March 19th need to be completed and/or demonstrated to be working.

(c)   Reports cannot be run from the Report Router.

(d)   Thirty reports have not been completed and of these, work has not begun on twenty- nine.

(e)   A User Guide for the AMS has not been delivered to CDA. There was no user documentation available to staff during acceptance testing. This made it difficult for the staff to test the system effectively and has prolonged the acceptance testing.

(f)   The acceptance testing has not demonstrated to the CEO and designated CDA consultants that the AMS software is performing at least adequately for the CDA to sufficiently use the AMS software for its operational requirements.

(g)   The training provided by MSI was not provided to a level where: (1) the Licensed Software could be demonstrated to operate as intended by the Functional Specifications, and (2) CDA staff could use the AMS software for its operational requirements.

(h)   Data cannot be exported to CDA's accounting system.

ACTIONS

(i)   MSI must provide CDA with a written plan to correct the deficiencies. MSI must restore the capability for CDA to resume its normal business operations within a timeframe that is acceptable to CDA at no extra cost. At the present time, the Association is not able to operate effectively and will not accept further delays in getting the AMS up and running. Effective immediately, CDA will begin documenting the cost of damages which are the direct result of MSI's substandard implementation.

(ii)   MSI must provide a report from Oracle that the recent upgrade has been installed correctly and that it should have resolved the current problems with generating WordPerfect merge reports.

II. Outstanding Contractual Obligations

MSI is obligated to perform or deliver the following per the Software Development and License Agreement:

(a)   demonstrate that the back-up is performing adequately

(b)   demonstrate that the AMS software performs the functions described under each menu item in Section 7 of Schedule "B" to the Agreement.

(c)   demonstrate that the AMS provides the data tables and data searches for two variables.

(d)   demonstrate a response time of less than 5 seconds for data searches for two variables.

(e)   demonstrate a response time of less than 5 minutes for the generation of reports which utilize two tables (maximum three pages).

(f) demonstrate that all reports described in the Functional Specification can be run and printed.

(g) demonstrate that the AMS provides effective linkages (export of data) to CDA's accounting system (AccPac).

(h) provide a detailed set of AMS software documentation:

– system administrator's guide

– user guide which meets specifications identified in the Agreement

– a copy of the source code of the AMS computer program, including: (i) file and database design structure, (ii) data dictionary, (iii) input/output design and (iv) program listings (hard and soft copies).

III. Performance Issues and Concerns

The overall implementation of the AMS project has not been handled satisfactorily. The resolution of ongoing problems has been costly and time consuming for both MSI and CDA. It has been hard for the staff to plan their time and much of the work performed each day has consisted of fighting fires at the last minute. The difficulties that CDA has encountered are summarized below and generally relate to the quality of MSI's project management and inadequate training.

<u>Project Management</u>

The implementation of this project has been rushed and has suffered from attempts to take short cuts. This is true for both the development work and the installation of the local area network. Decisions such as the one to deliver the AMS to CDA much too early caused confusion and disrupted CDA's operations unnecessarily. When the application was delivered, it was not useable and hardware could not be made available for both development work and training services.

MSI has not met the requirement for semi-monthly reports and three reports which were provided did not accurately reflect the status of this project. Many problems which should have been identified and brought to CDA's attention were addressed much too late or not at all. These include the delay in starting development work on reports, the loss of documentation needed by the programmers, and MSI's staffing shortage. In addition, MSI's decision to change the plan presented in its project report without consulting CDA was an unacceptable way of trying to make up time on the project.

It does not appear that much of the work required to complete this project has been carried out according to a well thought out plan. For example, it has been difficult to obtain timely information about tasks which needed to be handled by the staff, such as the table updates. If MSI had not been asked to update the staff, it appears that they would not have been given any direction along the way. The lack of timely instructions from MSI has left CDA with many empty tables, because there was not enough time for the staff to make the necessary decisions on what should be entered.

Poor planning was also evident in the area of training. Little or no time went into preparing for the staff training, On March 6th, (the first scheduled day of training) the session was cancelled. The cabling was not tested until Saturday, March 4th and was not in working order. When the training was delivered on March 7th, Patricia was told that the course material that was to be covered over a two day period was covered in one session.

Several times CDA's work has been put on hold because of MSI's commitments to other clients. This project has been negatively affected by the fact that MSI's Systems Analyst (Sean) has not had time to deliver services in a thorough manner, and we have not been able to count on him coming to the office as planned. The resolution of problems such as the AMS being down all day on May 1st and the loss of three applications which were installed on the network on April 30th have just had to wait until he could fit CDA into his schedule. No time seems to have been allowed for him to document the User Manual and System Administrator's Guide. His time constraints appear to have gone unnoticed and have not been addressed effectively with respect to CDA's needs.

Many activities have been carried out in a disorganized manner, because tasks have continually been left half finished. This has been particularly true of the LAN installation. Enough time was not allowed for the installation of hardware, software and related applications. Consequently, there have been numerous problems and Sean has spent an inordinate amount of time troubleshooting. This has left the users very frustrated with the new technology. External consultants have been brought in to evaluate the network, because the hardware environment has been so unstable.

When the installation is completed, MSI should provide a written report indicating that all activities listed on your December 19, 1994 fax have been completed. This report is necessary because the status of the LAN installation seems to fluctuate from day to day. In addition, time should be allocated for Sean to organize CDA's software and related documentation. The current condition of CDA's materials is not acceptable.

Another serious problem that required a significant amount of CDA's resources has been the fact that dozens of hours have had to be devoted to follow-up and research in order to resolve programming issues. There are three primary reasons for this.

First, CDA has been unable to rely on the information provided by MSI as to what would be included in the system. Last year, CDA paid to have three representatives of MSI attend a meeting to discuss the second draft of three Functional Specifications. The results of the meeting were not documented by anyone from MSI. Stephen has demonstrated a lack of knowledge about CDA's requirements. Every request for MSI to deliver what was promised has been treated as an opportunity for "extra billings". This required CDA to incur expenses to research each item to verify that it was in the Functional Specification.

When we meet this week, you should be prepared to explain why the March 14th Status Report says the Automatic Membership Cancellation Procedure is not in the Functional Specification or the information provided on CDA's Checklist, particularly since this formed part of the Software Agreement.

Secondly, it has been necessary to provide in-depth explanations of CDA requirements to the programmers. I assume this is due to your misplacement of the Entity Relation Diagram. This information has already been provided to MSI during extensive user interviews and several meetings where the draft Specification was discussed. A considerable number of hours went into repeating this information in order to resolve problems when the programmers had made incorrect assumptions about what was required. This is why CDA ended up with an inventory order form designed to support only over the counter sales. The programmer was not aware that CDA does not operate a cash and carry business out of its office.

Finally, Stephen appears to have the misconception that although CDA paid MSI $9,200.00 to translate the association's requirements into a Functional Specification document, CDA should bear some responsibility for the accuracy of the technical content. The fact that CDA didn't know that necessary tables and forms were left out should not justify extra billings to CDA. It was not CDA's role to verify your technical work.

Training

MSI did not deliver training at an acceptable level. It was difficult to obtain a written plan for the training and a complete plan has never been provided, although one was requested on February 16th and March 8th. Five sessions were cancelled on short notice. On at least two occasions, staff waited in the board room for over an hour before finding out that Sean would not be coming in that day. One of the reasons for cancelling the session was that he had to go to another client's site.

The staff sat through weeks of training without having the use of individual PCs, live data or any course materials. Both Stephen and Sean were advised more than once that the training was being delivered in an unacceptable manner. The situation with the PCs was brought to Stephen's attention the first time on March 8th. MSI's solution was to tell the staff not to worry because further training would be provided when the AMS was functional and the network was set up. Some staff were even told they didn't have to take notes. Matters were made worse by the fact that the association's busiest part of the season (membership renewal) was fast approaching.

The results achieved during the training sessions resulted in an extremely high level of frustration for the staff by the time the AMS could be accessed through the network. The initial testing was made even more difficult by the fact that the workstations were configured at different times and the information provided about the status of the network varied depending on who was asked about it.

The acceptance testing has been prolonged in part because of the poor quality of training and the fact that at least one-half of the staff did not have hardware that worked properly when the AMS could be tested. Progress reports were not provided as specified in the Software Agreement. Nor was the CEO advised that problems existed which would affect the implementation of acceptance testing.

Summary Comments

The current status of this project is completely unacceptable. Some of the AMS functions do work and the staff have received satisfactory training from the programmers; however, they are trying to perform their jobs using workarounds to problems. This cannot go on indefinitely. There is still a considerable amount of work to be done on this project. MSI needs to document a plan for completing this work in an acceptable timeframe. Please recognize that this situation is an urgent one and requires your full attention immediately."

The outcome of the meeting on May 11th was that the developer was allowed to go over budget. Marsha assumed the role of Project Manager. I continued to provide services to the CDA to help her with the transition at no charge to CDA. I had assumed that contract 72167 had been executed.

Exhibit Eight

The Board of Directors controls the performance of the CEO through its Policy Governance rules.

"Policy IV E

Executive Limitations Asset Protection (revised/approved by the Board of Directors February 20, 1994) forbids the CEO from binding the association through verbal agreements between the CEO and any person or organization."

Exhibit Nine

The CDA had to replace its computer system and computer equipment. The project involved developing a computer system that had limited access for the provincial associations and the CFDR.

I was in charge of finding a suitable software application. I managed the process of gathering information on user requirements for functional specifications, selecting a vendor to develop the new system and negotiation of a Software Development Agreement. The Functional Specifications Document and Agreement specified in detail the deliverables from the vendor. Markson Skolnik Inc. (MSI) was selected to develop a custom application for the association for $50,000.00.

Under the terms of contract 72850, I agreed to perform the work specified, i.e.:

(a)   between July 1 and September 30, 1994, supervise the development of on-line file look-up systems for policies file retention records, and operational procedures;

(b)   between July 1 and November 30, 1994, act as a liaison between CDA and Markson Skolnik Inc. during the initial programming phase of this project;

(c)   by September 30, 1994, document a proposal for external access to the national database which includes timelines and resource requirements (human and financial);

(d)   by September 30, 1994, identify special printing specifications for forms;

(e)   between December 1, 1994 and January 31, 1995, supervise testing of the system prototype with CDA staff and identify necessary screen format changes;

(f)   between December 1, 1994 and March 31, 1995, direct the Systems Analyst in developing a complete user guide based on CDA's internal operational procedures;

(g)   between January 1 and January 15, 1995, perform application testing with MSI on a test database and identify necessary programming changes;

(h)   between January 1 and February 15, 1995, assist with application testing using the entire database after conversion;

(i)   between February 1 and March 31, 1995, identify specifications for standardized reports to be created by the Systems Analyst; and

(j)   between July 1, 1994 and March 31, 1995, provide one project status update in person at the CDA head office and one written project status update to the CEO each month.

In addition to those tasks specified in the contract, as Project Manager, I was responsible for:

1)   verifying the accuracy of all invoices, i.e., ensuring duplicate invoices were not paid, that separate invoices for work covered by the developer's contract were not paid, and that all services listed on the invoices were delivered;

2)   working with the computer system programmers for up to nine hours per day. (This was necessitated by the fact that the Entity Relation Diagram was lost when the developer moved its office). Consequently, it was necessary for me to explain to the programmers on a daily basis the functionality required by the associations. At one point, the system had been programmed in a way that required the accounting staff to perform part of their work processing membership renewals manually. I worked with the senior programmer to re-program the system at no extra cost to the association.;

3)   meeting with thirteen staff of three organizations in groups and individually regarding reports they had requested (in excess of 40). Many hours of work were required because even though the staff wanted dozens of reports, they did not know how to formulate SQL statements and they could not identify what results they wanted to see on the reports. For example, a request was made for a report that would have printed out the entire database, when in fact the individual only wanted the names of a dozen or so members;

4)   resolving complaints and researching solutions to problems and alternative ways to provide the functionality the associations needed to have in order for the National Membership Management System to function as required;

5)   arranging for IT experts to give advice about technical issues and develop ad hoc solutions, e.g., meeting with the manager of the Canadian Foundation for Dietetic Research and a specialist on local area networks to determine how to link her database to the national database;

6)   following up daily with the developer regarding the status of the report software which did not work, and meeting with two new programmers that were hired April 2, 1995; and

7)   resolving staff performance issues daily, (many were related to the staff's lack of experience working in a Windows environment, lack of time to complete their regular work and train on the new system, and inadequate training delivered by the developer's Systems Analyst.)

EXHIBIT TEN

Every effort was made to resolve this matter without lengthy and costly litigation. W. Alex Kyle, solicitor, wrote to the CDA's Board of Directors to address the issue of the Plaintiffs' references.

Instead of providing the Plaintiffs with a good reference. "The Defendants stated that the Plaintiffs' actions were designed to harm the Defendants' reputation, frustrate the attempts of Marsha Sharp to follow her mandate from the Board of Directors and to further complicate and delay the completion of the installation of the computer system."

Mr. Kyle's letter reads as follows:

"July 7, 1995

The ... Association

Attention: Board of Directors

Dear Sirs/Madams:

Re: ...

Outstanding Account

I have been approached ... for the purpose of responding to the "Defendants' "letters of May 30, 1995 and June 21, 1995 from" the CEO ...

"In order to ensure that her work and company are not unfairly represented by "the CEO "in the future, "the Plaintiff" requests that a team of at least three Directors (to be mutually agreed upon by the Board and the Plaintiff) conduct a review of all work completed to date on Computer System and National Membership Management System projects. This request is being made because the Plaintiff's future employment prospects and ability to build her consulting practice could be adversely affected by the CEO's recent actions and written communications.

...I am advised that there is an unpaid account with the organization in excess of $12,000.00 "Please be advised that" the Plaintiff "is prepared to settle the payment of this account on the basis that the organization pay $11,980.79 for out-of-pocket expenses and the cost of professional services rendered to the organization during the period of May 8, 1995 through June 13, 1995. I understand that invoice number 6099 has been submitted directly to the Accounts Payable Department ... You may consider this letter as a demand for payment and an offer to settle pursuant to the Rules of Civil Procedure.

...

Yours truly,

Marler & Kyle
W. Alex Kyle

cc: Lynda Corby – President
Carollyne Conlinn – Past-President
Kathleen Morpurgo – President Elect
Elma Carson – Director, Manitoba
Carolyn Farris – Director, Alberta
Christine Gill – Director, Newfoundland
Martha MacLean – Director, New Brunswick
Debbie MacLlellan – Director, Prince Edward Island
Adele Mc Vicar – Director, Saskatchewan
Carol O'Fallon – Director, British Columbia
Jane Pryor – Director, Nova Scotia
Micheline Seguin-Bernier – Director, Quebec
Phyllis Tanaka – Director, Ontario"

KYLE LAW OFFICE
BARRISTER AND SOLICITOR

16-760 PACIFIC ROAD	W. ALEX KYLE	TELEPHONE 905.845-5000
OAKVILLE, ON L6L 6M5		FACSIMILE 905.845-5800
www.wakylelaw.com		wakyle@wakylelaw.com

FAX

TO:	June James	COMPANY:	
FAX NUMBER:	416-466-6781	DATE:	June 1, 2022
TIME:		PAGES:	1 (including this page)
FROM:	W. Alex Kyle	RE:	Letter of July 7, 1995
OUR FILE NO:	n/a	YOUR REFERENCE NO:	n/a

**In the event of transmission failure, please contact
Valerie Lloyd 905-845-5000**

Further to our telephone conversation of earlier this week, I confirm that I have no objection to you using my letter of July 7, 1995, a copy of which I understand is in your possession. As I warned you, due to the passage of time my file has been destroyed and therefore I cannot reproduce the letter for you.

W. Alex Kyle

Exhibit Eleven

Per my Letter of Engagement dated April 4, 1995, there were no tasks to be re-worked. The letter states:

"As Project Coordinator, I will handle the following tasks:

1.   Chair meetings of the Working Group and provide support to complete follow-up activities identified during the meetings.

2.   Monitor the status of activities assigned to team members with respect to meeting deadlines and advise the CEO of any missed deadlines.

3.   By January 31,1996, prepare a Policy Document for CDA which documents the historical development of the National Membership Management System, how the System will be maintained/updated on an ongoing basis and the decision-making process that has been agreed upon by all project participants.

4.   By January 31, 1996, document an evaluation process to obtain feedback from provincial associations on the quality of and member satisfaction with services provided by CDA under the national system."

Exhibit Twelve

In response to my solicitor's letter dated July 7, 1995, the Canadian Dietetic Association Board of Directors (per EXHIBIT TEN: Lynda Corby, Carollyne Conlinn, Kathleen Morpurgo, Adele Mc Vicar, Carol O'Fallon, Elma Carson, Carolyn Farris, Christine Gill, Jane Pryor, Phyllis Tanaka and Micheline Seguin-Bernier) voted unanimously to reject my offer to settle for $11,980.79.

The Board abdicated all responsibility for resolving the dispute by delegating control to Sharp, a staff employee reporting directly to the Board. Following is an excerpt from Sharp's letter per my affidavit of documents filed in Superior Court.

"July 17, 1995

Mr. W. Alex Kyle

Marler & Kyle

Barristers and Solicitors

…

RE: …

Dear Sir:

I have your letter of July 7, 1995. The CDA Board accepts the position I have and authorizes me to handle the situation. In future, please do not communicate directly or indirectly with the Board or any of its members. Your request for a Board review is without merit and inappropriate and therefore is refused.
…

Yours truly

Marsha Sharp"

Exhibit Thirteen

Under the terms of contract 60374, I agreed to perform the work specified, i.e.:

(a) between July 1 and July 31, 1994, document a national administrative plan specifying staff resources, shared costs, and basic operational procedures based on data received from each province;

(b) between July 1, 1994 and March 31, 1995 review procedural documentation developed with the Membership Marketing Coordinator and Accounting Clerk;

(c) between July 1, 1994 and March 31, 1995, act as a liaison between provincial representatives and CDA office staff;

(d) between August 1 and December 15, 1994, coordinate the production of membership materials;

(e) by November 30, 1994, document budget requirements for the 1995-1996 Fiscal Year;

(f) by March 31, 1995, document a post-mortem report as a reference document for processing memberships in the 1995-1996 fiscal year; and

(g) between July 1, 1994 and March 31, 1995, provide one project status update in person at the CDA head office and one written project status update to the CEO each month. The project reports were detailed monthly reports on the progress of the specifications in the contract. These reports were status updates for current tasks, future tasks to be completed and recommendations for relevant actions. Where appropriate, recommendations included alternative courses of action and selection of vendors.

Exhibit Fourteen

The following are excerpts from the Project Progress Report – October 27, 1994:

"The following is a report on the progress we have made to date toward the development of a National Membership Management System. The Master Plan of Action and related attachments have been updated and revised to reflect changes to deadline dates and work assignments. ... While some activities have not been completed according to our original schedule, our work is proceeding in a timely manner and we are still on target with respect to implementing the new system by January 1996.

1.   To date, we have received feedback on our Plan of Action from nine provinces. Nova Scotia has not responded yet. Melanie Reeves has reported that the ARDA (Alberta provincial association) has decided not to participate in this project for the time being.

2.   CDA is now processing blended student memberships for B.C. and Ontario, Georgette has completed an initial draft of the procedures for processing student memberships.

3.   CDA has engaged Pat as a Communications Consultant for the project. She will begin providing support for our communication activities in November.

4.   The Ontario Dietetic Association's (ODA) auditor has responded to questions about reporting and record maintenance requirements. The information provided by the auditor and ODA's responses are listed below. ...

5.   Ilona has been collecting information on current provincial legislative and By-law requirements. Team members should make every effort to submit their province's information by November 10th.

The above information is also relevant to the development of our new computer system. The actual programming will begin next week, so the information about membership categories that is gathered at this stage will help to ensure that we haven't missed any major computer system requirements in documenting the functional specifications.

6.   In response to our need for more factual information to help us determine exactly what amounts CDA should charge the provinces for membership processing fees. Marsha Sharp initiated a review of all current processing functions within CDA.

Exhibit Fifteen

August 12, 2019

FROM: Noie June James
Room 4- 157
3555 Danforth Avenue
Toronto, Ontario M1L 1E3

TO: Michael H. McCain, Chairman
Maple Leaf Foods Inc.
6897 Financial Drive
Mississauga, Ontario L5N 0A8

CC: NEWS...@citynews.ca
Business Editor, Toronto Star
1 Yonge Street
Toronto, Ontario M5E 1E6

Derek DeCloet, Business Editor
The Globe and Mail
351 King Street, Suite 1600
Toronto, Ontario M5A 0N1

RE: $50,000,000 DISPUTE WITH DIETITIANS OF CANADA (DOC) AND CANADIAN FOUNDATION FOR DIETETIC RESEARCH (CFDR)

I am requesting your help in resolving this dispute. I have enclosed copies of two books that I have written titled INJUSTICE and A Victim of Boards of Directors – Based on A True Story. Please take some time to read INJUSTICE. It will be obvious that I have been seriously mistreated...

...

My March 21, 2019 letter to the DOC and CFDR Boards details damages caused to my reputation. It should be noted that when I first realized that my good name was in jeopardy, I offered to settle the dispute for $11.980 to avoid serious damages to my reputation only five weeks into this dispute.

I have documented that I have a long history of excellent work. I have given the Boards copies of my documents, which include:

1.   performance evaluations with "very good" ratings;

2.   promotion announcements, i.e. four in six years I was promoted from branch management to software administration for all of Canada;

3.   a letter announcing that the Board of Directors of Hewlett-Packard (Canada) Ltd had awarded me thousands of dollars in stock options for my excellent work as a senior manager;

4.   performance rating of "exceptional" for completion of a $200,000 renovation project on budget;

5.   achievement of a 99.8% accuracy rate for an annual inventory count of computer parts valued at $750,000; and

6.   a copy of a business plan by a leading investment accounting firm in the amount of $480,000.

…

In closing, I hope you…help me get justice which is long overdue, since you have the capability to judge fairly whether or not my side of this dispute should prevail. The loss of my excellent reputation is invaluable. Thank you for considering my request.

Exhibit Sixteen

The Canadian Dietetic Association was established in 1935. The Dietitians of Canada was formed in 1997. The Canadian Foundation for Dietetic Research was created in 1991. Hundreds of individuals have been elected to the Boards of Directors for the three organizations.

To be nominated for positions on the Boards, applicants must demonstrate that they possess excellent communication and leadership skills, superior industry knowledge, professional expertise and strategic decision-making skills.

The following Board profiles are for past directors:
Specialties – Dietitians/Nutritionists profession at national and international levels; association development; management and executive leadership; working with Boards of Directors; partnership and alliance development and sustainability.

University education levels achieved:
PhD, MSc, MHSc, MA, BSc, RD

Internships: Completed at provincial hospitals

Employment history: Professors, Private Practice Consultants, Presidents of Corporations, Nutrition Educators, College Instructors, Research Scientists

Industry knowledge:
Reviewers of nutrition research - leaders and participants
National and international projects - focused on regulatory affairs in the food industry

Conductor of Dietetic Practice Based Research

Development of group-based education resources in the food industry

Educated in nutritional science

Exhibit Seventeen

The DC Board of Directors is made up of member volunteers who are elected and accountable to the DC membership. The Board devotes time, energy and talent to develop the strategic direction for DC and ensure that it remains strong, vibrant and relevant to our members and the profession.

The Board of Directors has adopted the "Policy Governance" model of governance. Working within a defined set of policies and by-laws, broadly the role of the Board is to:

- Set strategic priorities for the organization, to be achieved by the CEO
- Set boundaries, through policies, that describe conditions to be avoided by the CEO
- Assess CEO progress on priorities and monitors compliance with boundaries

More specifically, here are the responsibilities of the Board:

- Setting DC's long-range objectives and priorities.
- Assessing the degree to which plans and objectives have been achieved.
- Evaluating the performance of the CEO.
- Making decisions on operating budget.
- Making decisions on membership conditions and fees.
- Selecting the recipients of the Board award.

This Governance Process Policy describes the role of the Board in more detail.

The Ends Policies and Executive Limitations Policies provide the operating boundaries on matters the Board considers most important, such as treatment of staff, members, ethics, fees and more.

Exhibit Eighteen Profile

Violet Ryley and Kathleen Jeffs are renowned dietitians for their exemplary contributions to the advancement of the dietetic profession in Canada. The Ryley-Jeffs Memorial Award is the highest recognition that the Board of Directors of Canada can bestow on a member. It is given to individuals who exemplify the ideals demonstrated by two Canadian pioneers in the profession.

Marsha Sharp was honored in reflections from many Canadian and international colleagues. She was celebrated for leadership and advocating for dietetics around the world. As CEO of the Dietitians of Canada, she was dedicated to advancing the DC.

From 2016 to 2020, she was a director on the Board of the International Confederation of Dietetic Associations. She was appointed Board Chair. The ICDA is comprised of fifty-two associations around the world. Marsha represented the ICDA at meetings of dietitians/nutritionists in Asia, Europe, Middle East, and North America. She has worked with national dietetic associations in Africa and Australia.

Marsha's impressive achievements with extensive international and government contacts must have served to make her untouchable by Canadian Boards of Directors. She clearly achieved major successes in 1997, 2000, 2004, 2006, 2012, 2014, 2016, 2017, 2018, 2019 and 2020; however, while she was accomplishing laudable goals around the world during her thirty-three year career, she was also earning the complete support of three Canadian Boards of Directors to ruin my reputation and life.

Exhibit Nineteen

December 5, 2019
FROM: Noie June James
Room 4-157
3555 Danforth Avenue
Toronto, Ontario M1L 1E3

TO: Solicitor for Dietitians of Canada and Canadian Foundation for Dietetic Research
c/o 99 Yorkville Avenue, Second Floor
Toronto, Ontario M5R 1C1

CC: Business Editor
Toronto Star
1 Yonge Street
Toronto, Ontario M5E 1E6

Derek DeCloet
Globe and Mail
351 King Street, Suite 1600
Toronto, Ontario M5A 0N1

FYI ONLY: Michael H. McCain, Chairman
Maple Leaf Foods Inc.
6897 Financial Drive
Mississauga, Ontario L5N 0A8

RE: $150,000,000 Dispute with the Dietitians of Canada (DOC) and the Canadian Foundation for Dietetic Research (CFDR) for punitive damages

As you are aware, I have published a book titled, "A Victim of Boards of Directors – Based on a True Story". It is available from Amazon and through the publisher iUniverse. Over the last eight years, I have been contacted by over a dozen publishing companies and consultants regarding my contracting with them to create and manage marketing campaigns for the book.

Based on the significant national and international interest in marketing my book, I have agreed to write a third book titled, "A Victim of Boards of Directors II – Based on True Stories" bringing my second book up to date. My book "INJUSTICE" was not published, however it will greatly influence the content of my new book. The book will provide comprehensive exposes of everything I have lost and of the consequences I have suffered because of the numerous degrading actions of hundreds of directors over the last twenty-four and one-half years.

I have been in discussions with my publisher regarding guiding me with respect to the legal content of my new book based on their experience with "INJUSTICE", i.e. they will review my correspondence, court transcripts and the 400 plus supporting documents provided with my affidavits, all of which your clients possess. Given the inclusion of specific details in court files, i.e. the Statement and Amended Statement of Claim, and the Statement and Amended Statement of Defence and Counterclaims, I will take the opportunity to expand on the information in my earlier books. I will print: sworn statements recorded at the Examinations for Discovery, my letters to your clients (especially the one dated March 21, 2019), the information obtained from the internet about the directors of the DOC and the CFDR, names of news employees, news organizations that I have contacted about this dispute and information from my Admail document.

With respect to the information that is and has been posted to the internet, I will at least be able to print the details about Sharp and the national and international organizations, since the information is available from other sources. Copies of the information from the internet were sent to Michael McCain, Chairman of Maple Leaf Foods Inc. in August 2019. Several senior directors have been identified.

Your clients should note that I own the right to my correspondence which contains information that can be irrefutably proven to be true. They need to understand that my primary objective of my actions is to get justice. I am looking forward to printing information that the two Boards of Directors should have known was incompetent and meant to create acceptance of lies without question.

The solicitor I have chosen to represent me in case of a trial has advised me that I do not have to seek permission from the court to print any information verbatim from the documents we filed with the Superior Court because all of the documents are in the public domain. I can prove that a majority of Sharp's testimony on behalf of the DOC and CFDR at her Examination for Discovery on September 14, 2000 is testimony. In addition, the defendants' solicitor repeated testimony, saying "... My understanding is that it was a verbal agreement between June James and Marsha Sharp but that the verbal agreement in fact did reflect some of the proposals in the document numbered 72167."

The Boards of Directors have taken the position that all of the damages they are responsible for should be ignored because the statutes of limitations have expired for some of the detrimental actions. I disagree because the directors have a long history of defaming my reputation. It started in 1995 and continued with Marsha Sharp's tenure as Director of the CFDR. Two directors never spoke a word to me in twelve years and did not know me personally. Yet these directors with their Boards' approvals libeled me to two national multi-billion-dollar public corporations. They could only have done what they did with help. I had no knowledge of the executives the directors contacted for the sole purpose of compounding the damages the Boards had already inflicted on my reputation,

I contend that the Boards have never stopped communicating about this dispute to future Boards each year. The transcripts of their Board meetings would prove their guilt. Their only defence is to claim the transcripts are confidential or that making them public would harm the organizations. My new book will claim that the transcripts for the years 1995, 1996, 2000, 2004, 2010, 2017 and 2019 should be open to scrutiny, if the defendants are innocent of any wrongdoings. They shouldn't be allowed to hide behind the cloak of confidentiality to my detriment.

The Boards should worry about their reputations and costs to their stakeholders, if I am successful in having this dispute decided in the court of public opinion. I have suffered severe consequences and continue to do so.

…

My inclusion of information in court files and specific correspondence in my book is because of their probative value in demonstrating how hundreds of directors have engaged in long term cumulative patterns of abuse. One explanation as to why the Boards of Directors have accepted in silence public denouncements of their apparent support of defamation is that they are not legally required to respond to my letters, e.g. from 2010, 2017, and 2019. I don't believe silence will be an appropriate defence, when several of the chapters in my book are comprised of detailed texts from my letters. I have a right to suppose the wrongful behavior on the part of the directors in recent years is based on proven evidence of previous Boards of Directors having acted in concert to defame me.

…

In 1992, I was lead to believe that Marsha was only a CEO (an employee) reporting to a Board of Directors, formerly the Canadian Dietetic Association (CDA). In 1995, the CDA Board declined to take responsibility for settling this dispute with me and my company M-R Consulting (the name under which I was doing business). My book will include the letter dated July 7, 1995 verbatim from W. Alex Kyle to the Board of Directors, all of whom are named in the letter.

The Boards of Directors may want to hide their behavior, when it relates to Sharp's conduct. The lies in the court files and her testimony in the Examination for Discovery will demonstrate that Sharp may be incapable of telling the truth. Her letter dated July 17, 1995 speaks volumes about her ability to control other directors.

In 2017, my research on the internet revealed that Sharp was in fact one of the directors being sued. Since 1991, she held the titles of Founder and Director of the Canadian Foundation for Dietetic Research. Boards of Directors chose not to respond to my claim for damages and the fact that I hold the directors guilty for the damages. The directors continued supporting Marsha Sharp, and hundreds of directors have continued to support the ongoing defamation of my reputation without justification.

I have tried very hard to make the Boards of Directors understand the severe consequences that I have suffered at their hands. I came very close to committing suicide, because of the drastic loss of my excellent reputation, the unfathomable endless persecution and realization that my life was being ruined by dozens and later hundreds of individuals who were determined to destroy me for some unknown reasons, I have had to live with stress and depression for over twenty years.

In my March 21, 2019 letter to the Boards, I described in detail the toll their actions have taken on me physically and mentally over the years. After all my attempts in 2019 to try to make them act humanely, I have reached the conclusion that my book will enable me to finally achieve success and vindicate myself in the court of public opinion nationwide.

My new book will be much more explicit and thorough about details of this dispute from May 30, 1995 to the date of publication in 2020. This letter will be incorporated into my book, however, it doesn't begin to fully address the Boards' ongoing refusal to deal fairly with their long term systematic abuse of power. Based on the fact that I have the authority to print and name the litigants and actions described in public court documents and in my correspondence in my new book, your clients should consider settling this dispute before my book is published sometime between February 1 and March 31, 2020.

I have drafted thirty chapters of my new book so far and the reviews have been very positive. Based on how horribly I have been treated, I believe the Boards of Directors might rather gamble on their organizations suffering extreme negative consequences from adverse publicity, e.g. significant reductions in donations to the CFDR, than to admit what they have done wrong for twenty-four and one-half years.